FORGIVEN, FORGIVING, & FREE

DAN WINKLER

FORGIVEN FORGIVING AND *free*

THE PEACE OF LIVING WITHOUT A PAST

d&d PUBLISHING

ISBN-10: 069290980X
ISBN-13: 978-0692909805

Published by d&d publishing
Huntingdon, Tennessee 38344

Printed in the United States of America

Unless otherwise noted, all Scripture quotations are from The Holy Bible, English Standard Version®, copyright © 2001 by Crossway Bibles, a publishing ministry of Good News Publishers. Used by permission. All rights reserved. Scripture quotations marked NKJV are from the *New King James Version*. Copyright © 1979, 1980, 1982 by Thomas Nelson, Inc. Used by permission. All rights reserved.

Cover Design: Josh Feit, Evangela.com

CONTENTS

DEDICATION

To my dear mother, Betty Sue Winkler,
for the love you had for Daddy and for the many ways you
inspire, encourage, and prove that you love me.

PREFACE

F orgiveness seems thoroughly unnatural or inhuman. Americans believe in "justice for all" and value law and order. Whenever I have taught and counseled on forgiveness, many people have confessed to the seeming injustice of it all. When we forgive those who have wronged us, it feels like we are letting them off the hook, that justice isn't being done. Is forgiveness fair?

Forgiveness can also feel cowardly. Isn't it something only weak people do? It takes courage, we tell ourselves, to stand our ground and bear the standard of justice. Letting others off the hook for their sins is giving in; it's surrender. Is forgiveness for "snowflakes"?

I've discovered that these twin ideas—the "injustice" and "cowardice" of forgiveness—are more deep-seated than we imagine. Why else would we choose to live without forgiveness? Why would we decide to live without forgiving others, without forgiving ourselves, and without God's forgiveness so graciously offered to us in Christ? In Ephesians 4:31, Paul counseled us to unburden ourselves of bitterness, anger, malice, and the like, and to opt for forgiveness. Forgiveness makes life better; it is the antidote for all those things that make our lives toxic.

What you hold in your hands is an important book on a critical topic. It is, unequivocally, the best book on forgiveness I've ever read. Dan Winkler is known as a faithful, honest, and insightful student of God's Word. His ability to discern the truths of Scripture is rivaled only by his talent in communicating them. I first sat at his feet when I was sixteen; I listened to him expound the glorious truths of the New Testament Book of Hebrews for several hours and marked up my Bible as I listened. That was my first introduction to Dan Winkler—Student and Teacher of God's Word.

In the sixteen years since, however, I have come to know Dan as a person, a brother, a mentor, and a friend. We have observed and encouraged one another as we both walked the valley of the shadow of death. When my baby boy died, I called on him to preach the funeral, knowing that Dan knew all too well the pain of burying a precious son.

In fact, you should be aware that the words of this book flow from a heart and mind that has embraced forgiveness for many years, and to a degree beyond what you or I will ever approach. Dan Winkler is a person who has not merely considered forgiveness in the abstract; he has been forced to wrestle with, then embody it as the only way to live as God's child.

As you walk with Dan through this book and contemplate forgiveness, you will discover that forgiveness is not for weak people. Rather, forgiving yourself and others is among the most difficult things to do in life. And it also takes a tough, determined person to accept God's forgiveness. Forgiveness isn't for "snowflakes."

But you'll also discover that, yes, forgiveness is unjust. It is an erasure of our past, a banishment of our sins. Forgiveness is fundamentally unfair because it insists we not receive what we deserve. But when we fully recognize all the things we've done wrong, we wouldn't have it any other way.

It may be unnatural, but for the Christian, forgiveness is the only way to live.

— Michael Whitworth
Fort Worth, Texas

1

FORGIVEN BY GOD

The Peace of Living without Our Past

ionel was a bona fide serial killer. One of the best—I should probably say *one of the worst*. Three weeks after he graduated from high school, he murdered his first victim. Lionel was eighteen years old. He flayed the body, dissolved the soft tissue in acid, pulverized the bones, and spread them in the woods behind his parents' house.

It gets worse.

Over the next thirteen years, sixteen young men fell prey to Lionel's evil. He committed heinous acts of rape, murder, and necrophilia. The details of his crimes are so barbaric that I believe it would be too shameful to relate them. Suffice it to say he was nicknamed the "Milwaukee Cannibal." Lionel was finally arrested in the Summer of 1991 and sentenced to sixteen life terms in prison.

But that's only *part* of his story. Here's the rest.

Curt Booth was an uncle of my friend, Phil Sanders. In

Spring 1994, Curt saw Lionel interviewed on television. He had spent some time in prison himself and knew the difference Jesus can make in someone's life. He decided to send Lionel some reading material about the grace of salvation. Lionel was touched by the gesture, became interested in this magnificent message, and began to study the Bible with Roy Ratcliff, a minister in the churches of Christ. As a result of their weekly studies, in May 1994, Lionel assumed the fetal position in one of the prison's whirlpools and was baptized into Jesus.

Six weeks later, Lionel—Jeffrey Lionel Dahmer—was beaten to death by a fellow inmate. He died at the age of thirty-four. But he died as a brother in Jesus. He died without a past—*forgiven* by God!

That's what this chapter is all about. *We can know the peace that comes from living without a past.* No matter what you or I have done, no matter what we have allowed ourselves to become, God offers us the feelings of his heart.

You may be saying, "I haven't done anything half as bad as Jeffrey Dahmer." But that's the point. If God can embrace him—if he was willing to forgive Dahmer of all those violent, horrible things, don't you think he can forgive you?

We all have mistakes that haunt our memories. Some are secrets of shame, while others belong to a more public domain. Some are skeletons hiding in a closet. Others are skeletons dancing on a street corner, their bones rattling to capture the attention of everyone. What do your skeletons look like?

- The back seat of a parked car on a secluded path in

your high school days?

- The crude antics of a college sophomore during Spring Break?

- The exploits of a single adult tasting the dark thrills of a sordid night life?

- The escapades of a couple hiding amidst the anonymity of a vacation?

- The lies told and the people hurt to advance a career?

- The promises broken and the lives ruined by living for the moment?

- The bitterness that has been nurtured to a point of hatred?

- The hypocrisy of an empty soul hiding behind the façade of a full life?

We may never sink to the depravity of a Jeffrey Dahmer, but we have "all have sinned and fall short of the glory of God" (Romans 3:23). I have violated the will of God. I have been a disappointment to him. I may not believe myself to be a bad person, but I have done bad things. You have too. But here's the good news: God is willing to forgive us and free us from all the guilt of our past.

To help us take hold of this confidence, I want to ask four questions:

1.   What is forgiveness?

2.   Why are we forgiven?

3.   What happens when we're forgiven?

4.   How can we know we're forgiven?

WHAT IS FORGIVENESS?

I want you to write the word *forgiveness* on a sheet of paper. Now, mark through the first three letters of the word. Finished? Okay, mark through the last three letters of the word. It should look like this:

$$\text{F-O-R} \text{ G I V E N } \text{E-S-S}$$

There you have it. God's forgiveness is the greatest gift man has ever been given. Consider the two words used in the New Testament for *forgiveness*.

To be forgiven is to be *graced* by God. One of the New Testament's words for *forgiveness*, *charizomai*, is akin to the Greek word *charis*, which means *grace*. It is used in Ephesians 4:32 when Paul speaks of how "God in Christ *forgave* you" (emphasis mine). When God forgives us, what he's really doing is treating us with grace! What an amazing thought!

Think for a moment of *grace* as a recipe with three special ingredients. All three ingredients are involved when God forgives our past. In the following passage, note how many times you read the word *grace*, and circle each one:

But God, being rich in mercy, because of the great love with which he loved us, even when we were dead in our trespasses, made us alive together with Christ—by grace you have been saved— and raised us up with him and seated us with him in the heavenly places in Christ Jesus, so that in the coming ages he might show the immeasurable riches of his grace in kindness toward us in Christ Jesus. For by grace you have been saved through faith. And this is not your own doing; it is the gift of God.

Ephesians 2:4-8

Now, read those words again, only this time, underline the words *mercy, love,* and *kindness.* Those are the three ingredients that create God's grace.

- **Mercy** *is a part of God's grace.* It's the part that moves God to feel *with* us. He is "rich in mercy" and wants to enrich our lives with the forgiveness of his heart (Luke 6:36).

- **Love** *is a part of God's grace.* It's the part that moves God to feel *for* us. Because he loves us with such a "great love," he is willing to offer us the forgiveness of his heart (1 John 4:7).

- **Kindness** *is a part of God's grace.* It's the part that moves God to reach out and feel *toward* us, to be good to us and give us the forgiveness of his heart (Romans 2:4).

Isn't that wonderful? When God forgives us, he is sympathizing with us, lovingly reaching out to us, and helping us with our past. Doesn't that make you want to worship "with thankfulness in your hearts to God" (Colossians 3:16)?

But wait—there's more!

To be forgiven is to have something *erased* by God. The other New Testament word for *forgiven* is *aphiemi*, a combination of the Greek *apo*, meaning *away*, and *hiemi*, meaning *to send*. Together, *aphiemi* means *to send away*.

That's what God does when he forgives; he graciously reaches out to us with his heart and throws away our sins. David summed it up well by writing, "as far as the east is from the west, so far does he remove our transgressions from us" (Psalm 103:12). God "is faithful and just to forgive us our sins [i.e., send away our sins] and to cleanse us from all unrighteousness" (1 John 1:9).

Think of how big God's heart has to be to do something like that.

- *When we sin, we **FIGHT** with God.* That's what *transgression* means: rebellion (Psalm 5:10; Hebrews 3:16-18). It's a clenched fist we shake in God's face.

- *When we sin, we are **FILTH** before God.* That's what *iniquity* means: perversion (Leviticus 18:24-25; 19:8; Job 33:27). It's conduct that makes us twisted and perverted in God's eyes.

- *When we sin, we are **FAILURES** to God.* That's

what *sin* means: missing the mark God has set for us to attain (1 John 5:17; James 4:17). It's a life that is anything but what God wanted for us.

But when God forgives, he throws all that away and allows us to start over with life. He looks at us and says, "This person 'is a new creation. The old has passed away; behold, the new has come'" (2 Corinthians 5:17). It's almost too hard to believe, but it's true!

WHY ARE WE FORGIVEN?

Why is God willing to treat us like this? When we are forgiven, God treats us like we've never made a bad decision. It's like we've never failed to do what he commands. It's as if we've never done what he told us not to do. He graces us with his heart and throws away our past. But why? Why is he so willing to do something like that? The answer has two sides.

To begin, we need to realize that we are not forgiven *because of who we are*. None of us are *good enough* to deserve God's mercy and love. None of us have *done enough* to earn God's kindness. We never will. We could do everything we have been commanded to do, and we would still be forced to say, "We are unworthy servants" (Luke 17:10).

Rather, we are forgiven *because of who God is*. Look at the way God spoke of himself before giving Moses a second copy of the Ten Commandments:

The LORD, the LORD, a God merciful and gracious,

slow to anger, and abounding in steadfast love and
faithfulness, keeping steadfast love for thousands,
forgiving iniquity and transgression and sin…

Exodus 34:6-7

First, God identified himself as "the LORD, the LORD."
Literally, his words mean, "I am that I am, I am that I am" or "I
will be who I will be, I will be who I will be" (Exodus 3:13-14).
It's as if God introduced himself by saying, "Moses, I want you
to really think about who I am."

**Second, God described himself as "a God merciful and
gracious."** To be merciful is to step inside the skin of another
and feel what they feel. To be *gracious* is to act on those feelings
and reach out to help another. Couple that idea with the repeat-
ed use of *LORD*, and you have: "I am that I am, I am that I am, a
God that feels with you and reaches out to you." Wow!

Third, God specified why he is willing to forgive. He is
"slow to anger, and abounding in steadfast love and faithfulness." That means he doesn't lose his temper. He has deep feelings for us, and he always will.

Forgiveness is something beautiful that happens inside the
heart of God because God is the kind of God he chooses to be.
He is a God that is always "ready to forgive" (Nehemiah 9:17).

WHAT HAPPENS WHEN WE'RE FORGIVEN?

The newspaper tycoon William Randolph Hearst called
Arthur Brisbane, "the greatest journalist of his day." Brisbane's
syndicated column boasted a readership of some twenty mil-

lion. But Brisbane, this man of words, is the one who said, "Use a picture. It is worth a thousand words."

That's what God has done throughout the Old Testament. He has painted pictures—word pictures—to help us better understand forgiveness. Let's look at five and string them together to see why we should appreciate this wonderful gift.

1. Forgiveness involves a *COVERING.*

> Blessed is the one whose transgression is forgiven,
> whose sin is covered.
>
> Psalm 32:1

If you owed a debt in ancient times, the amount you owed would be etched on the surface of a stone or piece of pottery. When the debt was paid, melted wax would cover the etching to prove you no longer owed the debt. That's the idea behind David's reference to *covered* sin. Our sins are a debt we owe to God, and every one of them has been scratched onto the surface of a stone that represents our past (Matthew 6:12). Our words (Matthew 12:37). Our indifference (Matthew 25:41-45). Our deeds (Romans 2:6-11). Our secrets (Romans 2:16). They're all there. Personally, I fear it would take a rock quarry to chronicle all of mine. How about yours?

But when God forgives our sin-debt, he covers over every one of those etchings with something far more precious than wax. Our sins are covered with the blood of Jesus. "In him we have redemption through his blood, the forgiveness of our trespasses, according to the riches of his grace" (Ephesians 1:7; cf. 1 John 1:7).

2. Forgiveness involves a *CARVING*.

> Come now, let us reason together […] though your sins are like scarlet, they shall be as white as snow; though they are red like crimson, they shall become like wool.
>
> Isaiah 1:18

In this passage, the Hebrew word for *scarlet* means "double-dyed," the word for *red* means "blood-red," and the word for *crimson* refers to a color that came from dried, crushed insects. Because we sin, we look like we have been double-dipped in some kind of bloody bug extract. We're stained and defiled (Jeremiah 2:22)—what a disgusting image.

With forgiveness, we are just the opposite: "white as snow." The blood of Jesus bleaches our souls clean (Revelation 1:5; 7:14). If we compare our past to an engraved stone that has been covered by the blood of Jesus, this passage suggests that God carves away the etchings and scrapes the stone smooth. He makes it look like nothing was ever etched there in the first place (Psalm 51:7).

3. Forgiveness involves a *CASTING*.

> In love you have delivered my life from the pit of destruction, for you have cast all my sins behind

your back.

Isaiah 38:17

When we sin, we do more than just turn our backs on God. We throw him and his Word behind our backs (1 Kings 14:9; Nehemiah 9:26; Psalm 50:17). We forcibly put what God wants behind us in favor of our own seductive desires (James 1:14-15). And if we think of God at all, it's only as an afterthought.

With forgiveness, God takes the stone that represents our past and tosses it behind his back as if to say, "I have no interest in this" (cf. Psalm 51:9). God turns his back on our sins; when he forgives, he has no interest in what we've done in the past (Hebrews 10:17). None!

4. Forgiveness involves a *CLOUD*.

I have blotted out your transgressions like a cloud and your sins like mist; return to me, for I have redeemed you.

Isaiah 44:22

Sin is like a thick cloud standing between and separating us from God (Isaiah 59:1-2). He hates it (Proverbs 8:13) and is so disgusted by it that he turns his face away from us when he sees it in our lives (Psalm 51:9).

With forgiveness, the warmth of his grace forces that cloud to dissipate and exposes us to his favor once again. That means, when God throws away the stone representing our past, wherever it falls, he causes it to explode into oblivion. Our past is gone; our record is expunged; our sins are blotted out (Psalm 51:1, 9).

5. Forgiveness involves a *CONCEALING*.

Who is a God like you, pardoning iniquity and passing over transgression [...] You will cast all our sins into the depths of the sea.

Micah 7:18-19

Oceanic trenches are yawning, narrow depressions across the ocean floor. One of these is the Mariana Trench east of the Philippines. It's 1,580 miles long, 43 miles wide, and almost 2½ times as deep as Pike's Peak is tall. It's the deepest hole on earth that we know about, and it serves as a great example of what Micah called "the depths of the sea."

With forgiveness, God has promised to "put away [our] sin" (2 Samuel 12:13), and guess where it goes. The stone that represents our past is thrown behind God's back where it falls into the deepest parts of the sea and explodes into nonexistence, never to be thought of again. There is no way to thank God enough for that!

HOW CAN WE KNOW WE'RE FORGIVEN?

All sorts of answers have been suggested. Some make it harder to enjoy God's grace than it really is. They may not be quite as bad as the Jews who required circumcision and a strict obedience to the Old Testament (Acts 15:1), but they're not far behind. To them, salvation comes in *cans* with *labels*. They will tell you what you "can" do or "can't" do and "label" you if you don't comply. Listen to them, and you'll want to ask with the disciples, "Who then can be saved?" (Matthew 19:25).

Others try to make it easier to know God's favor than it really is. Some claim you just need to accept a thought. Others urge you to say a particular prayer. Do that, and you're saved. But you won't find an example of anyone doing that in the New Testament and becoming saved as a result.

"Do this."

"Don't do that."

"You have to..."

"You don't really have to..."

Sound confusing? Why don't we allow God to speak for himself on this subject? Let God tell us what's needed to be welcomed into the forgiveness and favor of his heart. If we listen, we will hear him give attention to four key words.

BIBLE. According to God, the Bible is necessary for our forgiveness. It "is not in man who walks to direct his steps" (Jeremiah 10:23). Trying to get to heaven on our own is like driving blindfolded through a traffic jam in the middle of rush hour. By ourselves, it's impossible to find the way out of our treacherous past into the safety of God's presence.

We need to be saying what David said, "Teach me to do your will, for you are my God! Let your good Spirit lead me on level ground!" (Psalm 143:10). The gospel is "the power of God for salvation" (Romans 1:16). It's the message that will "save [our] souls" (1 Corinthians 15:1-2; cf. James 1:21). We must allow the Bible to tell us what to do to be forgiven by God.

BLOOD. According to God, the blood of Jesus is necessary for our forgiveness. He tells us that "without the shedding of blood there is no forgiveness" (Hebrews 9:22). Yet, "it is impossible for the blood of bulls and goats to take away sins" (Hebrews 10:4). Old Testament sacrifices don't work anymore. Today, we come into God's presence "by the blood of Jesus" (Hebrews 10:19). Think about these amazing ideas and carefully read these Scriptures:

- *Justification*—being just-as-if-I'd never sinned. "Since, therefore, we have now been *justified* by his *blood*, much more shall we be saved by him from the wrath of God" (Romans 5:9; emphasis mine).

- *Redemption*—being purchased by and belonging to God's mercy. "In him we have *redemption* through his *blood*, the forgiveness of our trespasses, according to the riches of his grace" (Ephesians 1:7; emphasis mine),

- *Reconciliation*—being united and at peace with God again. "For in him all the fullness of God was pleased to dwell, and through him to *reconcile* to himself all things, whether on earth or in heaven, making peace by the *blood* of his cross" (Colossians 1:19-20; emphasis mine).

- *Remission*—being freed from the past. "Jesus Christ [is] the faithful witness, the firstborn of the dead, and the ruler of kings on earth [...] who loves us and has *freed us* from our sins by his *blood*" (Revelation 1:5; emphasis mine).

- *Sanctification*—being set apart as special to God. "How much worse punishment, do you think, will be deserved by the one who has trampled underfoot the Son of God, and has profaned the *blood* of the covenant by which he was *sanctified*, and has outraged the Spirit of grace?" (Hebrews 10:29; emphasis mine).

- *Salvation*—being confident of our eternal destiny. "Now the *salvation* and the power and the kingdom of our God and the authority of his Christ have come, for the accuser of our brothers has been thrown down […] And they have conquered him by the *blood* of the Lamb and by the word of their testimony, for they loved not their lives even unto death" (Revelation 12:10-11; emphasis mine).

Every one of these blessings is made possible by "the precious blood of Christ" (1 Peter 1:18). It is his blood that grants us access into and keeps us in a wonderful state of forgiveness (1 John 1:7).

BELIEF. According to God, believing in Jesus is needed for our forgiveness. One of the most familiar verses of the Bible says, "For God so loved the world, that he gave his only Son, that whoever believes in him should not perish but have eternal life" (John 3:16).

Jesus said it himself, "I told you that you would die in your sins, for unless you believe that I am he you will die in your sins" (John 8:24). His best friend, John, teaches us to "believe that Jesus is the Christ, the Son of God […] that by believing [we] may have life in his name" (John 20:31). Faith in Jesus is essential to our being forgiven by God and living with him forever.

BAPTISM. According to God, being baptized is also needed for our forgiveness. Those who believed Peter's sermon at Pentecost were told, "Repent and be baptized every one of you in the name of Jesus Christ for the forgiveness of your sins" (Acts 2:38).

Some claim that "for the forgiveness of your sins" in this verse means I must be baptized *because* my sins have been forgiven. Others say that those words mean I must be baptized *so that* my sins *can be* forgiven. The first idea makes baptism an *expression* of forgiveness. The second makes it a *condition* of forgiveness. Which is it?

What Saul was told to do clarifies things for me: "Rise and be baptized and wash away your sins, calling on his [i.e., the Lord's] name" (Acts 22:16). For Saul, as well as you and me, baptism was something necessary in order to be washed clean and forgiven. Is there something special about the water? Absolutely not. Is it the physical act of washing with water that saves? No (1 Peter 3:21).

We are saved and forgiven (1) according to the teaching of the **BIBLE** (2) by the **BLOOD** of our Lord (3) when we **BELIEVE** in him (4) with a faith that moves us to be **BAPTIZED**. How wonderfully simple that is! Bible. Blood. Belief. Baptism.

They're all a part of this beautiful process that results in our past being totally abolished.

A fter correcting a misspelled word with his big eraser, a first grader asked his teacher, "Where do mistakes go when you rub them out?" Great question!

Where do our mistakes go when God wipes them out? The Bible says they're sent into a blank void of nonexistence. We are forgiven and blessed to live at peace with our past. To put that another way, we are blessed to live in peace without a past.

In the words of Horatio Spafford's great hymn, "It Is Well with My Soul"—

My sin—oh, the bless of this glorious thought!
My sin, not in part but the whole,
Is nailed to the cross, and I bear it no more,
Praise the Lord, praise the Lord, O my soul!

2

FORGIVING MYSELF

The Peace of Living with Our Past

We put ourselves down because we're damaged goods. We've been "damaged by the decisions of our past." We beat ourselves up because we have "a history that is no mystery" to others. We can't hide our past, but even worse, we can't hide *from* our past.

The emotional strain is awful; the spiritual strain, devastating. No matter how much we believe in God's mercy, it can be difficult to *feel* forgiven.

There's a reason. We don't feel forgiven because we haven't forgiven ourselves! That's what this chapter is about. *We can get past the past.*

Let's begin with what we'll call "The Parable of the Backpack."

Each of us has a backpack. The first thing we want to do is turn the front panel of our packs inside out and embroider a single word on the inside. Each of us will use the same gaudy gray thread and stitch the same word. Others won't be able to read the word. They won't know what it says. When we're finished and turn the panel right side out, all they'll be able to see is a wadded mess of threads from the word we stitched on the inside. Here's the word we're going to sew into the panel.

G U I L T

The next thing we are going to do is put as many big rocks as we can inside our backpack—*really* big rocks. Once we've stuffed our packs with big rocks, let's pour gravel into the empty crevices that remain. Now, zip up your pack, put it over your shoulders, and carry it around all day long. I'll do the same.

Nobody knows what's on the inside. They have no idea how heavy our pack is or how long we've been carrying it. All they can see is the emotional wreck we have become from toting that stuff around. We're physically exhausted and emotionally spent. And we keep carrying that pack around, all the while wondering why we can't just take it off and leave it behind. Here's the point of the parable:

- The backpack symbolizes our emotions.

- The rocks and gravel are the sins of our past. Some of them are whoppers, with consequences to match. Some are less consequential, but they're still sin.

- The word we sewed, G-U-I-L-T, is how we feel about those sins.

- The mess of threads that others see represents the mood swings, disappointments, worry, and resentment that come from our feelings of remorse.

- Finally, the weariness that comes from carrying all this guilt is the shame we want to escape.

Get the picture? We all have rocks in our backpacks. What do yours look like?

- The financial mess that made you sign bankruptcy papers?

- The memories of premarital sex you dragged into your adulthood?

- The extramarital rendezvous that has haunted your insomnia?

- The private encounters you have shared with on-line porn?

- The reputations you brutally slaughtered with your gossip?

- The bottle you've hidden in or tried to hide too often to remember?

- The drug paraphernalia that seductively whispers your name?

- The raw deal that made you money at the expense of another?

- The eating disorder that ravaged a body you wish

looked differently?

How can we live with stuff like that? How can we forgive ourselves for being like that? If we are willing to take three very simple steps, we might be able to *come to grips* with a past that *has a grip on us*. We must be willing to:

1. Accept God's love,

2. Believe God's promises, and

3. Trust God's grace.

STEP #1: ACCEPT GOD'S LOVE

Contrite is a synonym for guilt. It comes from a Latin word that means "ground down," and that's pretty much what guilt does. It makes us feel like our hearts have been pushed through a meat grinder with questions of shame coming out the other side. *Why did I do that? What was I thinking? Who all knows? Where do I go from here?*

Here's the problem with all of that: we are thinking too much of self. We are thinking more about the one who needs forgiveness than the one who forgives! To forgive ourselves, we must see ourselves through God's eyes and allow ourselves to be loved by him.

A string of Old Testament statements might help. Did you know that guilty feelings draw God to us like a magnet? Look at these verses:

The LORD is near to the brokenhearted and saves the *crushed* ["contrite," NKJV] in spirit.

Psalm 34:18; emphasis mine

The sacrifices of God are a broken spirit; a broken and *contrite* heart, O God, you will not despise.

Psalm 51:17; emphasis mine

For thus says the One who is high and lifted up, who inhabits eternity, whose name is Holy: "I dwell in the high and holy place, and also with him who is of a *contrite* [literally, "crushed"] and lowly spirit, to revive the spirit of the lowly, and to revive the heart of the *contrite*.

Isaiah 57:15; emphasis mine

This is the one to whom I will look: he who is humble and *contrite* [literally, "crippled"] in spirit and trembles at my word.

Isaiah 66:2; emphasis mine

God's heart gravitates to us when our hearts are broken by sin. Isn't that wonderful? *Feeling bad* about sin is a *good feeling*. Paul calls it "godly grief" (2 Corinthians 7:10-11). God not only gives us his attention when we feel this way; he showers us with his affection.

A special New Testament story might also help. It's a story about a son's guilty feelings and a father's love (Luke 15:11-32). We usually call it "The Parable of the Prodigal Son," but it's not really about the son. It's about the boy's father. It's not about the son's guilt. It's about the father's grace. It's really a story about our heavenly Father's grace and the love he has for us when we feel guilty.

The story opens with the sins of a selfish son. They were doozies (vv. 11-13, 30). By demanding his inheritance, the son treated his daddy like he was already dead. He stormed through life in what Jesus called "prodigal" (or, more literally, "unsaved") living. His brother even accused him of pandering with prostitutes.

As the story continues, the boy's sins were very destructive (vv. 14-17). We might say he lost his money to casinos, canteens, and call girls. He lost his buddies to hard times. He lost his dignity to the task of sloppin' hogs that ate better than he. How appropriate. He had become unclean in his ways and was forced to spend his days with unclean animals (cf. Leviticus 11:4ff; Deuteronomy 14:3ff).

The thought of his mistakes finally overpowered this son with guilt and depression (vv. 18-19). He thought about how he had been cared for in his father's house, and then he looked around at the mud and mire of the pig sty he was caring for. In the midst of all this filth and want, he realized what he had lost. "I have sinned [...] and am no longer worthy."

The story climaxes with the love of a merciful father. Look at what this father *did* (v. 20). The father "saw" his son from a long way off and recognized the silhouette of someone he loved. He "ran" to, embraced, and kissed his son. Then, he interrupted the boy's self-debasing words, "I am no longer worthy." He wouldn't even let him finish his well-rehearsed speech. Instead, this father believed in second chances. Our heavenly Father does too.

> Therefore, if anyone is in Christ, he is a new creation.
> The old has passed away; behold, the new has come.
>
> 2 Corinthians 5:17

Look at what this father *felt* (vv. 20-23). The father was "moved with compassion" because of what he saw. He "kissed" his son, and the word Jesus used meant he "intensely loved" his son. Then, he rejoiced in treating his son with favor: "Let's eat and celebrate." Did you know that our heavenly Father has a heart just like that?

> Who is a God like you, pardoning iniquity and passing over transgression for the remnant of his inheritance? He does not retain his anger forever, because he delights in steadfast love.
>
> Micah 7:18

Look at what this father *said* (vv. 24-32). He ordered his servants to clothe his son in the best robe, a ring, and shoes—all gestures of affection (cf. Ezekiel 16:6-14; Genesis 41:42; Zechariah 3:3-5). He honored the boy with a feast, saying, "For this my son was dead, and is alive again; he was lost, and is found" (Luke 15:24). The sinner was treated as if he had never done anything wrong. That's how our heavenly Father treats us when we're forgiven.

> For I will be merciful toward their iniquities, and I
> will remember their sins no more.
>
> Hebrews 8:12; cf. 10:17

If God's love for us is that great, if his treatment of us is that gracious, shouldn't we be gracious with ourselves? If we want to forgive ourselves, we must be willing to filter our feelings about self through the heart of God. We must allow ourselves to be loved by God and start loving ourselves again!

STEP #2: BELIEVE GOD'S PROMISES

Are you saved? Do you feel saved? Do you believe in the promises God made to the saved? If you're *right* with God, shouldn't you feel *alright* about yourself?

The Bible is very clear in its teachings about the conditions *for* salvation. Some things are absolutely essential. To begin, God's grace is essential. His feelings for man made our salvation *available* (Ephesians 2:8). Without his mercy, love, and kindness, none of us would have any hope (Titus 3:3-7). Still further, the blood of Jesus is essential. It made salvation *accessible* (Ephesians 2:13; cf. 1:7). We can be justified (i.e., just-if-ied never sinned) because of the blood that flowed from Jesus' side (Romans 5:9). Finally, our faith is essential. A faith like Abraham's—one that accepts what God says, trusts in what God says, and acts on what God says—has made salvation *applicable* to each of us (Romans 4:19-5:2).

The Bible is equally clear in its teaching about the condition *of* salvation. We can know we are in a saved condition. At least three men were inspired by the Holy Spirit to record this kind of confidence. First, there was Paul. He was so assured of his salvation that he wrote about the "crown of righteousness" he was going to receive from Jesus (2 Timothy 4:8). Second, there was Peter. He felt so prepared for the salvation he would receive at Jesus' return that he was "looking for and hastening the coming of the day (2 Peter 3:12-13). Third, there was John. He was so confident of his eternal destiny that he attached to Jesus' last words—"Surely I am coming soon"—the prayer, "Amen. Come, Lord Jesus" (Revelation 22:20).

These same three men who were so confident of their own salvation were also used by the Holy Spirit to tell us that we can enjoy the same peace of mind they possessed. What a blessing that is in our times of doubt and weakness!

Listen to Paul:

> There is therefore now no condemnation to those who are in Christ Jesus, who do not walk according to the flesh, but according to the Spirit.
>
> Romans 8:1 NKJV

When? Now.

What? No condemnation.

Who? Those who are in Christ, following the Holy Spirit's teachings.

You mean we can know that we are not going to hell? Yes! Shouldn't that help us feel better about ourselves? We're not lost!

Listen to Peter. After encouraging us to have faith, virtue, knowledge, self-control, steadfastness, godliness, brotherly affection, and love, he went on to write:

> For if these qualities are yours and are increasing
> [...] if you practice these qualities you will never
> fall. For in this way there will be richly provided
> for you an entrance into the eternal kingdom of our
> Lord and Savior Jesus Christ.
>
> 2 Peter 1:8-11

You mean we can know we are going to heaven? Yes! And again, that assurance should make us feel better about ourselves! We're not lost; we're saved!

Listen to the apostle John. He wrote to those of us that have already been forgiven and reminds us that we can live with a remarkable peace of mind. If we walk with God, Jesus' blood continues to keep us clean. We stay in a perpetual state of forgiveness!

> But if we walk in the light, as he is in the light, we
> have fellowship with one another, and the blood of
> Jesus his Son cleanses [literally, "keeps on cleans-
> ing"] us from all sin.
>
> 1 John 1:7

You mean we can know that we are not going to hell; we can know that we are going to heaven, and we can know all of that while we're still on earth? Why wouldn't we feel good about ourselves? We're forgiven of our past, continually cleansed in the present, and we live with the joy of heaven in our future.

Years ago, I heard of an older preacher trying to help a man struggling with his faith in prayer. The preacher challenged this man to go out into the seclusion of a nearby forest and, in his solitude, curse God. The man was horrified with the idea and the preacher replied, "There you go. You believe that God will hear you when you curse him, but you don't believe he hears you when you pray."

We need to take that to our own feelings of guilt. We believe that a faithful God will record our sins and punish us. So why aren't we willing to believe that a forgiving God will remove our sins and keep his promise? If a sin is forgiven, it's gone. If it's gone, it's not there. If it's not there, we shouldn't be thinking about it. God doesn't. Why fret over something that doesn't exist? Believe what God has promised!

STEP #3: TRUST GOD'S GRACE

Our feelings of guilt must be replaced with God's feelings of grace. We might not be able to *forget* the past, but we don't have to *fret* over it. That's a lesson we can learn from two of the worst sinners to ever live. And no, I'm not being judgmental; that's the way they described themselves.

First, there is David in the Old Testament. He's the one that prayed:

> O my God, in you I trust […] Turn to me and be gracious to me, for I am lonely and afflicted. The troubles of my heart are enlarged; bring me out of

my distresses. Consider my affliction and my trouble, and forgive all my sins.

Psalm 25:2, 16-18

"Lonely." "Afflicted." "Troubles." "Distress." "Affliction." "Trouble." David felt crushed beneath the weight of his guilt. But look what he did. He prayed for God's forgiveness and took refuge in God's grace.

The background of all this drama is rather appalling. Uriah was one of David's "mighty men" (2 Samuel 23:39), one of his best soldiers. But while this good man was off fighting for his king, his king was back home committing adultery with the man's wife, Bathsheba. He even got her pregnant and tried to hide their indiscretions. He called Uriah in from the battlefield, lied to him, got him drunk, and encouraged him to go home and have sex with his wife. That way, everyone would have thought that Bathsheba's baby was Uriah's. But Uriah refused, and David had his loyal servant placed on the front lines where, by design, he was killed in battle. Now, let's see. There was a sex scandal, a government cover-up, and a covert plan of murder-by-proxy. Today's politicians would have to work hard to top all of that.

Uriah was wronged and never knew it. But God knew it. He sent his prophet, Nathan, with a message that forced David to face the shame of his guilt (2 Samuel 12:9-12). Psalms 51 and 32 are thought to be the result of this encounter. Pause for a moment and read these two psalms. The first pleads for forgiveness; the second offers praise for forgiveness.

As you read Psalm 51, look at the grief that came from David's feelings of guilt. He felt:

- "Defiled" and unclean (vv. 1-3)
- "Degraded" and evil (vv. 4-6)
- "Devastated" and broken (vv. 7-9)
- "Dismissed" and severed from God (vv. 10-11).

David felt the full weight of the sin that had caused so much damage, but there was no way to undo his actions. He couldn't change the past, but he could choose how to face his present. So, what did David do? He pled for God to have "mercy" and treat him with "lovingkindness" (Psalm 51:1 NKJV). He asked for grace.

Now, read Psalm 32 and look at the relief that came from God's forgiveness and grace. Right in the middle of the psalm, David tells us what he did with his guilt. "I acknowledged my sin to you, and I did not cover my iniquity; I said, 'I will confess my transgressions to the LORD,' and you forgave the iniquity of my sin" (v. 5). He replaced his feelings with God's feelings, and the results were transforming. That is why the psalm begins and concludes with words of joy:

> Blessed is the one whose transgression is forgiven, whose sin is covered. Blessed is the man against whom the LORD counts no iniquity, and in whose spirit there is no deceit. [...] Many are the sorrows

of the wicked, but steadfast love surrounds the one
who trusts in the LORD. Be glad in the LORD, and
rejoice, O righteous, and shout for joy, all you up-
right in heart!

Psalm 32:1-2, 10-11

The relief that came from a belief in God's mercy helped
David forgive himself and get past his past.

Second, there is Paul in the New Testament. Paul had
a hard time moving beyond his violent history. He spoke or
wrote about it all the time. For example, he's the one that said,
"I persecuted [Christians] to the death, binding and delivering
to prison both men and women" (Acts 22:4). And again, "I not
only locked up many of the saints in prison after receiving authority from the chief priests, but when they were put to death
I cast my vote against them. And I punished them often in all
the synagogues and tried to make them blaspheme, and in rag-
ing fury against them I persecuted them even to foreign cities"
(Acts 26:10-11).

On another occasion he wrote, "For I am the least of the
apostles, unworthy to be called an apostle, because I persecuted
the church of God. But by the grace of God I am what I am" (1
Corinthians 15:9-10; cf. Galatians 1:13-15, 23). Paul hated the
sin of his past, but he knew that he was loved by God, and that
lifted him above his past.

Read the words he wrote to Timothy and take note of the
five things Paul did to invite God's grace into a life soiled by
bad decisions.

I thank him who has given me strength, Christ Jesus our Lord, because he judged me faithful, appointing me to his service, though formerly I was a blasphemer, persecutor, and insolent opponent. But I received mercy because I had acted ignorantly in unbelief, and the grace of our Lord overflowed for me with the faith and love that are in Christ Jesus. The saying is trustworthy and deserving of full acceptance, that Christ Jesus came into the world to save sinners, of whom I am the foremost. But I received mercy for this reason, that in me, as the foremost, Jesus Christ might display his perfect patience as an example to those who were to believe in him for eternal life. To the King of the ages, immortal, invisible, the only God, be honor and glory forever and ever. Amen.

1 Timothy 1:12-17

First, Paul talked to Jesus and thanked him for the blessings of his grace (v. 12). Isn't that a super idea? If you want to rise above the rubble of your past, make a list of how the Lord has changed your life and, at least once a day, thank him for something on that list.

Second, grace kept Paul from being harder on himself than he had to be (v. 13). He owned his past as a "vocal" blasphemer, a "vicious" persecutor, and a "violent" opponent of Christianity. He didn't suppress the memory. He didn't blame someone else for his decisions. He wrote about the ugly part of his past and then, without pause, focused on the beauty of God's heart.

That's another great point for us to remember. By the grace of God, we are better people than we used to be. I love this little saying:

> I may not be what I want to be;
> I may not be what I am going to be;
> But, thank God, by his mercy,
> I am not what I used to be.

Third, Paul emphatically pointed to grace as the blessing that changed his life. He said, "the grace of our Lord overflowed for me" (v. 14). Paul was raised by a great family (Acts 23:6). He went to the best schools (Acts 22:3), and he was even at the head of his class (Galatians 1:14). But Paul believed that he was who he was because God is who God is, a God of grace. If you and I want to come to terms with our past, we need to do like Paul: look *up*, not *back*.

Fourth, Paul talked about Jesus' grace (vv. 15-16). He saw himself as a showcase of grace. "Christ Jesus came into the world to save sinners," he wrote, "of whom I am the foremost. But I received mercy for this reason, that in me, as the foremost, Jesus Christ might display his perfect patience." Paul had come to know God's mercy, and he couldn't quit talking about it. Wow! You and I might think a little less about our days-gone-by if we talk more about God as this day goes by.

Finally, Paul took the time to praise God for his grace (v. 17). In this same passage, he broke into one of the richest expressions of worship found in all of his letters. Look at how he *de-*

scribed God: "eternal," "immortal," "invisible." Look at what he *ascribed* to God: "honor and glory and forever and ever." As if "honor" wasn't enough, he added "glory." Then, as if honor and glory" weren't enough, he added "forever." And even more, as if "forever" wasn't long enough, he doubled it, "forever and ever." Then, he attached a closing exclamation mark: "Amen!" Do you want to learn how to forgive yourself? Set aside time in the day, find a place to be alone, and sing a song that praises God for the wonder of his grace. Then, pray a prayer of thanksgiving for the joy of your salvation. It'll help you overcome your past by directing you to the multitude of blessings you enjoy today.

L et's return to the Parable of the Backpack. Are you tired? Are you weary from the grind of carrying around all those rocks?

WHAT ROCKS? Remember, when God forgives us, he thinks of us as if our past is gone. To him, there are no rocks to carry around, big or small. That means the burden of guilt we are trying to carry around is nothing more than the product of an overly sensitive imagination.

I'm not trying to make light of where we've been, what we've done, or who we might have hurt along the way. I'm trying to remind us that we are loved by a God who has promised to save us by his grace. I'm trying to get us—to borrow a phrase from Scripture—to "no longer have any consciousness of sins" in our past. They're not there (Hebrews 10:2).

Hallelujah!

3

FORGIVING OTHERS

The Peace of Living with Others in Our Past

Anyone. *Anything.*

Those are the two most challenging words Jesus ever spoke. Put them back into the verse where Jesus used them and see if you don't agree.

> And whenever you stand praying, forgive, if you have anything against anyone, so that your Father also who is in heaven may forgive you your trespasses.
>
> Mark 11:25

Forgive anyone? Some folks are easy to forgive. Those we love. Those who have forgiven us. Those we don't have to be around much. But according to Jesus, we must be willing to forgive *anyone.* What about those we don't like? What about those that don't like us? *Anyone!?*

Forgive anything? Some things are easy to forgive. Little mistakes. Minor infractions. Things that make us say, "Oops," instead of, "Oh!" But Jesus calls us to forgive *anything*. What about those things we can't look over because they seem to take over our lives? What about the wounds that won't heal or the scars that won't fade? *Anything!?*

How do we get over:

- a body ravaged by another's reckless decision?
- a betrayal of being lied to or about?
- a love lost to the lust of a seductive touch?
- a promotion stolen by stealth or greed?

How can we forgive stuff like that? It has to be possible or Jesus wouldn't have said, "Be merciful, even as your Father is merciful. […] Forgive, and you will be forgiven; give [in context, this means "give another your heart"], and it will be given to you" (Luke 6:36-38).

This chapter is a tough one. It's all about doing something we might not want to do. *It's about making peace with those that forced us to piece our lives back together.*

We might not want to forgive. We might find it painful to revisit a place we never wanted to be in the first place. We might find it distasteful to think about someone we want to forget. But that's what true forgiveness is all about. We have to forget the *something* that was done to us and not the *someone* that did it. To help us do that, let's spend a little time with:

1. One observation,

2. Two suggestions, and

3. Three conditions of a heart willing to forgive.

ONE OBSERVATION

Forgiveness is hard.

I love the little boy's prayer: "Lord, forgive us our trash baskets as we forgive those who put trash in our baskets." I know. Jesus actually said, "If you forgive others their trespasses, your heavenly Father will also forgive you" (Matthew 6:14). But there are times when I feel like others have thrown a whole lot of trash in my basket. And I don't always feel overly gracious about it. Can you relate?

Do you remember when Jesus wanted to know which was easier, to say, "Your sins are forgiven," or, "Rise and walk" [i.e., to perform a miracle] (Matthew 9:5)? Sometimes I think a miracle would be easier than mercy.

- Easier to walk on water than to walk away from what another has done to you

- Easier to raise the dead than rise above what another has said.

- Easier to restore a withered hand than extend a hand to the one that hurt you.

- Easier to feed five thousand with a lunch sack than help some "sad sack" that didn't care how they made you feel.

It's hard to give the fragments of your heart to the one that broke it! It's *hard*.

There are some Bible "exhortations" that point to the difficulty of forgiving others. In fact, every member of the Godhead has something to say about this.

For example, our heavenly Father has taught us to replace feelings of animosity with affection for those who mistreat us: "You shall not take vengeance or bear a grudge [...] but you shall love your neighbor as yourself: I am the LORD" (Leviticus 19:18; cf. 1 Thessalonians 4:9; James 2:8). Why would he say something like that if anger and resentment weren't so natural and forgiveness so hard?

Still further, Jesus has taught us to do whatever it takes to get along with those who mistreat us: "Do not resist the one who is evil. But if anyone slaps you on the right cheek, turn to him the other also. And if anyone would sue you and take your tunic, let him have your cloak as well. And if anyone forces you to go one mile, go with him two miles" (Matthew 5:39-41). Why would he emphatically say the same thing three different ways if retaliation wasn't so easy and forgiveness so hard?

And then the Holy Spirit has taught us to be kind to those who mistreat us: "Beloved, never avenge yourselves [...] To the contrary, 'if your enemy is hungry, feed him; if he is thirsty, give him something to drink; for by so doing you will heap burning coals on his head.' Do not be overcome by evil, but overcome evil with good" (Romans 12:19-21). Why would he prohibit vengeance and promote benevolence if wanting to "get even" wasn't so natural and forgiveness so hard?

There are also some biblical examples of people who struggled with the idea of forgiving others. They were good people who were serious about their relationship with God, but they found it very difficult to have a relationship with those that hurt them.

Peter is the first that comes to mind. He is the one that asked, "Lord, how often will my brother sin against me, and I forgive him? As many as seven times?" (Matthew 18:21). Maybe he had the book of Proverbs in mind. It reminds us that "the righteous falls seven times and rises again" (Proverbs 24:16). Maybe he was thinking about the rabbis of his day who, based on the words of Amos, believed in forgiving someone else three times (Amos 1:3, 6, 9, 11, 13; 2:1, 4, 6). Jesus' answer must have seemed a bit radical: "I do not say to you seven times, but seventy-seven times" (Matthew 18:22).

The other apostles found it difficult as well. Jesus said, "If your brother sins, rebuke him, and if he repents, forgive him, and if he sins against you seven times in the day, and turns to you seven times, saying, 'I repent,' you must forgive him." When the apostles heard that, they said, "Increase our faith!" (Luke 17:3-5).

And what about the Christians in Corinth? They were severely rebuked for not correcting one of their members who repeatedly had sex with his father's wife (disgusting, I know). Still, it happened, and Paul instructed the man's fellow Christians to chastise him (1 Corinthians 5). Apparently, they did what Paul told them to do (2 Corinthians 7:8-12), but caring for this sinner proved to be more difficult than correcting him.

Paul had to tell them to "forgive," "comfort," and "love" the man to keep him from being swallowed up by his shame (2 Corinthians 2:4-8).

Thanks be to God! You and I are normal in this regard. Some who were far more spiritual than we didn't find it so easy to forgive. They struggled to work through the pain and bitterness just like the rest of us. Forgiveness is hard. But it's not impossible.

TWO SUGGESTIONS

To be *unforgiving* is to be *unforgiven* because "judgment is without mercy to one who has shown no mercy" (James 2:13). There is no way to be right with God if we are not going to forgive and do right by others.

Forgiveness helps us to be "imitators of God" and "walk in love" (Ephesians 4:32; 5:2). Forgiveness helps us to be more like Jesus, who prayed from the cross, "Father, forgive them, for they know not what they do" (Luke 23:32). Forgiveness also helps us to be what the Holy Spirit teaches us to be: "compassionate" and "forgiving" (Colossians 3:12-13). So even though it is tough, we need to work at it. Thankfully, Jesus gives us two suggestions that can help.

> Again I say to you, if two of you *agree* on earth about anything they ask, it will be done for them by my Father in heaven. For where two or three are *gathered* in my name, there am I among them.
>
> Matthew 18:19-20; emphasis mine

Look at our Lord's words "agree" and "gathered." They make forgiveness possible.

First, Jesus teaches us to "talk with" the person that needs our forgiveness. The word he used for "agree" (Greek *sumphoneo*) is a compound of two Greek words: *sun*, "together," and *phoneo*, "to sound" (we get our English *symphony* from this word). The idea is that of two people sounding out their differences.

Look at the verses just before this idea. Jesus tells us how to come together and discuss our past (Matthew 18:15-17).

a. We are to start by talking to the person that hurt us.

b. If that doesn't work, we are to take someone with us and try to talk with them again.

c. If that doesn't work, we are to solicit the help of the church.

d. Then, if that doesn't work, we are to walk away from our relationship with the offender.

We are to talk *with* each other, not *about* each other if we want to be forgiving. When we do this, four words need to serve as guideposts:

- *Hear.* Listen to each other. Have open minds.

- *Honest.* Be truthful with each other. We can't read each other's minds.

- *Humble.* Be kind to each other. Avoid giving each other a piece of our minds.

- *Helpful.* Think of solutions for each other. "Great minds think alike."

Second, Jesus teaches us to "walk with" the person that needs our forgiveness. The word he used for "gathered" is the Greek *sunago*. Like the Greek word for "agree," *sunago* is a compound Greek word of *sun*, "together," and *ago*, "to go." Thus, the word means two or three "going together," (cf. "synagogue," a place where ancient Jews would go and meet together). The picture Jesus painted is amazing. Those of us in conflict with one another need to talk through our differences and, from that point, live together as if those differences never existed.

That's what God does when he forgives. He treats us as if we've never done what we've done (Hebrews 8:12), and we are to forgive each other the same way God forgives us (Ephesians 4:32). That means we are to forgive each other and treat each other as if what was done had never been done at all.

I told you this was a tough chapter. But don't quit reading. Don't give up. Don't say, "I can't do that," or "I don't want to do that." There's a story coming up that teaches us exactly what we need to do to make this happen.

THREE CONDITIONS

Forgiveness is a very special gift from a very special heart. That's the point Jesus made in one of his most famous illustrations, the Parable of the Unforgiving Servant (Matthew 18:23-35). Look at the closing line of this story: You will know the wrath of God "if you do not forgive your brother from your heart." Three dramatic scenes lead up to this conclusion.

Scene #1: A "Pardon" (vv. 22-27). A servant owed his king "ten thousand talents." God only required three thousand talents of gold and five thousand talents of silver to build Solomon's Temple (1 Chronicles 29:3-5). This man owed a staggering ten thousand talents and couldn't pay it back. In desperation, he begged, "Have patience with me." But instead of patience, his master was moved with compassion and gave him a pardon. He asked for an "I-owe-you," but his master gave him a "paid-in-full."

Scene #2: A "Plea" (vv. 28-31). A second servant owed the forgiven servant "a hundred denarii," one hundred days' worth of wages (Matthew 20:2). He could have paid off that amount in a few months, but he also pled, "Have patience with me." This time, instead of patience or pardon, the indebted was sent to prison. The man who had been forgiven was unforgiving. Treating someone else like that is horrifying. But there's more.

Scene #3: A "Punishment" (vv. 32-35). The unforgiving servant was forgiven a debt that was more than the combined annual taxes of Judea, Samaria, Galilee, Idumea, and Perea. Still, he was insensitive to someone that owed him just a few dollars by comparison. The result? His king was angered, called him "wicked," and "delivered him to the torturers." Why? He had been shown mercy, but had refused to show mercy.

So what kind of heart makes forgiveness easier?

First, we need a heart of "patience" if we want to be forgiving. Both servants in Jesus' story said, "Have patience with me," or, more literally, "be long in getting angry with me." That means if we want to be more forgiving, we'll have to work on our temper. The Holy Spirit is pretty empathetic about this. We must *suffer long with those who make us suffer.*

> Good sense makes one slow to anger, and it is his glory to overlook an offense.
>
> Proverbs 19:11

> Whoever is slow to anger has great understanding, but he who has a hasty temper exalts folly.
>
> Proverbs 14:29

> A hot-tempered man stirs up strife, but he who is slow to anger quiets contention.
>
> Proverbs 15:18

Second, we need a heart of "compassion" if we want to be forgiving. The king of Jesus' story was "moved with compassion" and forgave. The prefix *com* suggests a degree of "togetherness" and, of course, *passion* involves the idea of "strong emotions." So if we want to be forgiving like this king, we'll have to turn away from our own hurt feelings and try to feel with the one that hurts us. We need to be asking: *Why did they do what they did? What were they feeling? If we traded places, would we feel the same way?*

Finally, all of you, have unity of mind, sympathy, brotherly love, a tender heart, and a humble mind. Do not repay evil for evil or reviling for reviling, but on the contrary, bless, for to this you were called, that you may obtain a blessing.

1 Peter 3:8-9

Third, we need a heart of "mercy" if we want to be forgiving. In place of "mercy," some translations use the word "pity." Again, the king of Jesus' story described his forgiveness by saying, "I had mercy on you." The word translated "mercy" carries the idea of helping someone that needs something from us like the blind men (Matthew 9:27; 20:30-31) or the desperate parents (Matthew 15:22; 17:15) who cried to Jesus.

In summary, to be forgiving, we are not to get mad when others hurt us. Instead, we are to see life from their perspective and do what we can to help them. Before you think that's impossible, revisit Jesus' beatitudes. Each of them begins with the Greek word *makarioi*, meaning "blessed" or "happy." Here are three relate to our trying to make the best out of a mess someone else has made of our lives.

Blessed are the meek, for they shall inherit the earth.

Blessed are the merciful, for they shall receive mercy.

Blessed are the peacemakers, for they shall be called sons of God.

Matthew 5:5, 7, 9

Do you want to be happy? Be "meek" or gentle. Don't be bitter and angry with the one that hurt you. Be "merciful. Try to feel with the one who hurt you. Be a "peacemaker." Do all you can to work with the one who hurt you.

One year, while visiting Washington, DC, I found a museum that gave attention to the death of Abraham Lincoln. I got to see the flag that served as a pillow for his wounded head. Under glass, I saw the contents of his pockets the night he was shot, his overcoat, and yes, his iconic top hat. I couldn't believe I was seeing this with my own eyes. I felt like a little boy with a $20 bill in a candy store.

The most impressive sight of this self-guided tour was a tower of books inside a spiral staircase. This tower was above five feet in circumference, three stories tall, and was built out of every book that had been written about our sixteenth president. He is a man we remember with great respect, and I think I know at least one of the reasons why.

Edwin Stanton was Lincoln's legal and political rival. On one occasion, he even called Lincoln a gorilla and a clown. But after being elected president, Lincoln chose Stanton to be his Secretary of War. Others were astonished and wondered how the president could be so forgiving. According to Lincoln, the appointment was granted because he thought Stanton was the best man for the job. Of interest, after the dreadful events of April 14, 1865, it was Stanton that stood by the lifeless body of his president and said, "Now he belongs to the ages."

Nothing we do will impact others more than our willingness to forgive. Yes, it's hard! It's hard—but worth every effort. Who knows? Maybe, just maybe, if you and I are willing to welcome another back into our wounded heart, someone might say of us one day: "Now they belong to the ages." After all, forgiveness is a *chance to change the past*.

4

FORGIVING GOD

The Peace of Living with Our Broken Past

It was the most compelling photo I saw after 9/11. What made it so compelling? It wasn't a landscape of carnage and death. It wasn't a portrait of some brave first-responder fighting through the day's confusion. It wasn't a snapshot of a Good Samaritan reaching out to another. For me, that awful day was best captured by the shot of an ambulance.

In the background, you could see what was left of the World Trade Center. In the forefront, there was an emergency vehicle coming up to a traffic light. The light was green. Not red for *STOP* or yellow for *CAUTION*. It was green for *GO*.

The symbolism was hard to miss. When your world crumbles, you might want to *STOP* and put everything on hold. In times of emergency, the *CAUTION* of a paranoid imagination might cause you to second guess every decision you have to make. But sooner or later, you have to pick yourself up, push yourself forward, and *GO* on living your life. I know. Believe me; I know. It's not easy.

When life gets hard—when life hurts—we usually want to hide and wonder if God is on our side. We want to put things on pause and look for a cause.

I want to ask you two very personal questions. I want you to be brutally honest in your answer.

Question #1: *Have you ever been disappointed with God?*

Has he ever let you down? Has he ever said "No!" to a selfless request? Ever made you wait for something you asked? From your perspective, has God ever failed to be there for you when you needed him most?

That's how Job felt. Job wanted to complain. He felt like he had the right to fuss; that he had a legitimate beef. He said, "I will not restrain my mouth; I will speak in the anguish of my spirit; I will complain in the bitterness of my soul" (Job 7:11). But he couldn't find God anywhere, and that frustrated him to no end.

> Today […] my complaint is bitter; my hand is heavy on account of my groaning. Oh, that I knew where I might find him, that I might come even to his seat! I would lay my case before him and fill my mouth with arguments. […] I go forward, but he is not there, and backward, but I do not perceive him; on the left hand when he is working, I do not behold him; he turns to the right hand, but I do not see him.
>
> Job 23:2-9

David felt the same way. On one occasion, he asked God the same question four times: "How long?" Later, he had the nerve to challenge God: "Consider and answer me." David was beside himself. He felt abandoned and, like most of us, wanted answers. Can you sense his despair?

> How long, O LORD? Will you forget me forever? How long will you hide your face from me? How long must I take counsel in my soul and have sorrow in my heart all the day? How long…?
>
> Psalm 13:1-3

Jesus felt the same way. In Gethsemane, "with loud cries and tears," he begged the Father to save him from Golgotha (Hebrews 5:7; Luke 22:39-44). But even to Jesus' plea, God said "No." Thus, while on the cross and feeling more alone than anyone else has ever felt, our Lord shouted,

> My God, my God, why have you forsaken me?
>
> Matthew 27:46

That is, "Why have you let me down in this?"

So if you have ever felt like God wasn't there for you, you're in pretty good company.

Question #2: *Have you ever been disappointed with life?*

Have you ever had your heart broken by someone you loved? Have you ever been betrayed by someone you trusted? Ever been left with the scars of a memory you wish you could forget? Has life ever been less than you planned?

I wonder if Adam felt disappointed. He named his wife *Eve*, which means *living*. Adam couldn't have been happier than the day God put Eve in his life. But she's the one that invited death into the world (Genesis 2:16-17; 3:20-24). Eve is the reason Adam was expelled from Eden and forced to struggle through life (Genesis 2:23; 3:17-24). Do you think Adam might have been disappointed at times?

I wonder if Rachel felt disappointed. When God finally blessed her with a child, she named him *Joseph*, which means, "the LORD shall add to me another son." God did, but the birth of that second boy cost Rachel her own life, and she died naming that second son *Ben-oni*, "son of my sorrow" (Genesis 30:24; 35:18). Again, that sounds like an expression of great disappointment.

I wonder if Joseph felt disappointment. Granted, years after his brothers' mistreatment, he said, "Do not fear […] you meant evil against me, but God meant it for good" (Genesis 50:19-20). Still, what went through his mind when his brothers sold him into slavery at the age of seventeen? What did he think when he was falsely accused of rape and unjustly imprisoned? There was a time when he said to his cellmates, "I was indeed stolen out of the land of the Hebrews, and here also I have done nothing that they should put me into the pit" (Genesis 40:15). That sounds like disappointment to me.

Unfortunately, these two questions are often strung together. Life doesn't turn out the way we thought, so we turn on God because he didn't do what we thought he should. We cry and want to know why:

- God, why did this happen if you're really there? Aren't you in control?

- God, why did this happen if you really care? You do, don't you?

- God, why do you let bad things happen to good people?

- God, why do you let good things happen to bad people?

- God, why, *why* did you let this happen to *me*?

Why did they have to die in that car wreck?
Why was she raped?
Why was their house blown away?
Why did they both lose their jobs—and in the same month?
Why was he falsely accused and imprisoned?
Why the cancer?
Why only months to live?
Why?

Many of us have been forced into those dark places, and we want answers. Speaking with respect, we want God to explain himself. We might even be upset with him.

That's what this chapter is about. *We need to forgive, or not blame, God for our problems. Rather, we should try to understand why he allows us to suffer.*

Think with me about three three-letter words: *man, God,* and *joy.* These three words can help us see our *past* as a *cast* that can mold us into someone better. These three words can help us understand the place suffering plays in making us all we can be for God's glory.

MAN

Let's return to the story of Job. That poor man lost almost *everything* and *everyone* in his life. He was left with a wife that wanted him to curse God and a few "friends" that thought God cursed him (Job 1:13-20; 4:7; 7:3-7; 11:3-5).

Job is the one that asked, "What is man, that you make so much of him, and that you set your heart on him, visit him every morning and test him every moment?" (Job 7:17-18). Paraphrased: "What have I done to deserve all this attention from God? Why is he treating me this way?" What is man? Here are four answers that can help us understand who we are and help us see why God allows us to hurt.

Man is fragile. In a sense, we are designed to be damaged. It only takes one of our one hundred billion nerve cells to remind us of this. We break. We ache. We die, and all because we are not made of steel or stone. We are "flesh and blood" (Hebrews 2:14). We suffer because we are "frail" (Psalm 39:4 NKJV). Why did God make us fragile or capable of being damaged? As Paul puts it:

> Though our outer self is wasting away, our inner self is being renewed day by day. For this light momentary affliction is preparing for us an eternal weight of glory beyond all comparison, as we look not to the things that are seen but to the things that are

unseen. For the things that are seen are transient,
but the things that are unseen are eternal.

2 Corinthians 4:16-18

According to Paul, we are unseen, spirit beings living in-side transient bodies that are wasting away. God made us this way because, in his judgment, the suffering that comes from this combination can prepare us for something better. God doesn't want to *hurt* us. He wants to *help* us. So he allows us to struggle through trials *here* to prepare us for something far more glorious *hereafter*.

Man is volitional. We all have voices in the choices we make. We are free moral agents, meaning we are free to be an agent of things immoral. We can refuse or choose whatever we wish, but consequences are sure to follow. Remember Paul's warning? "Whatever one sows, that will he also reap" (Gala-tians 6:7). If we use our freedom of choice to make good de-cisions, the results are generally positive. If we decide to make bad choices, the results can be painful. That's another reason why we struggle with life. We hurt ourselves. It's not God's *fault*, but our own *failures*, that make us suffer.

Man is social. We are wired to network. Like grains of salt, we season each other's life (Matthew 5:13; Mark 9:50; Colos-sians 4:6). Like flames of light, we shine on one another's path (Matthew 5:16; Philippians 2:14-15; 1 Peter 2:9). We're not sol-itary telephone poles in the middle of a pasture. We're fence posts linked together. If one post is knocked down; if one rots and weakens, those posts closest are affected. There are times when we struggle with life because "none of us lives to himself, and none of us dies to himself" (Romans 14:7). When someone we love hurts, we hurt *with them* (Romans 12:15). When someone we love hurts us, we hurt *because of them* (2 Timothy 4:10).

Man is pliable. We are clay in the hands of a master craftsman. God is the potter, life is the potter's wheel, and our problems are the molds by which he shapes us into something beautiful. "For the moment," we are told, "all discipline seems painful rather than pleasant, but later it yields the peaceful fruit of righteousness to those who have been trained by it" (Hebrews 12:11). We are allowed to suffer because God knows that *bad things* aren't all *bad*. I remember pumping iron when I was younger. When you push through the pain of lifting weights, you're tearing muscle fibers. When the fibers heal, the muscle is stronger, bigger. You break down your muscles to build them. That's what God does when he allows us to hurt. Struggles *break us down* and, if used properly, *build us up*. In our weakness, we are made stronger. It seems like someone else said that—Paul.

> So to keep me from becoming conceited [...] a thorn was given me in the flesh, a messenger of Satan to harass me, to keep me from becoming conceited. Three times I pleaded with the Lord about this, that it should leave me. But he said to me, "My grace is sufficient for you, for my power is made perfect in weakness." Therefore I will boast all the more gladly of my weaknesses, so that the power of Christ may rest upon me. For the sake of Christ, then, I am content with weaknesses, insults, hard-

ships, persecutions, and calamities. For when I am
weak, then I am strong.

2 Corinthians 12:7-10

GOD

We just looked at Job's question, "What is man?" Now, let's
look at a question Pharaoh asked Moses, "Who is the LORD?"
(Exodus 3:2).

Who is God? His personal name is *YHWH* (Exodus 6:3).
That's a theonym some call the tetragrammaton. It is the four
consonants God used for his covenant name. It means, "I AM
WHO I AM" or "I WILL BE WHO I WILL BE" (Exodus 6:14).
We could say that God is who he has been, who he is, and who
he is going to be.

But what is God like? That's the question we should really
ask if we want to know why we hurt. Here are four answers that
might help us appreciate God more deeply and better understand why he allows us to suffer.

God is exceptional. His "greatness is unsearchable" (Psalms
145:3; cf. 104:1). God's judgments are great (Psalm 36:6), his
works are great (Psalms 92:5; 111:2), his love is great (Psalm
117:2), his mercy is great (Psalm 119:156), and there is absolutely no measure to his great glory (Psalm 138:5).

God is everywhere at the same time. "O LORD, you have
searched me and known me! You know when I sit down and
when I rise up; you discern my thoughts from afar […] and
are acquainted with all my ways. […] Where shall I go from
your Spirit? Or where shall I flee from your presence?" (Psalm

139:1-3, 7).

God sees everything that goes on. "The LORD looks down from heaven; he sees all the children of man; from where he sits enthroned he looks out on all the inhabitants of the earth, he who fashions the hearts of them all and observes all their deeds" (Psalm 33:13-15). His eyes "are in every place, keeping watch on the evil and the good" (Proverbs 15:3).

God knows everything there is to know. There is not a language he can't speak, a discipline he hasn't mastered, or an equation he can't solve. He knew the details of relativity and quantum physics before they were even discovered. His "understanding is beyond measure" (Psalm 147:5; cf. Romans 11:33).

Put all these thoughts together. When we give God our problems, he knows who we are and all we are going through to survive life (cf. Matthew 6:8).

God is eternal. He is "from everlasting to everlasting" (Psalm 90:2; cf. Isaiah 40:28). He lives inside of eternity (Isaiah 57:15; cf. 1 Kings 8:27). Try wrapping your mind around that! He is the "Lord God Almighty, who was and is and is to come!" (Revelation 4:8; cf. Deuteronomy 33:27; Romans 16:26)!

There is not a problem we face that God hasn't already addressed. Anything we experience, God has already worked through in someone else's life (Ecclesiastes 1:9). I find that comforting. God knows who we are, what we're going through, and as the "God of all comfort," he knows how to help us (2 Corinthians 1:3-4).

God is powerful. He is "exalted in power" (Job 37:23; cf. Revelation 19:6 NKJV). Nothing is "too hard" for him (Jeremiah 32:17; cf. Genesis 18:14) and "all things are possible" with him (Matthew 19:26). He "is able to do exceedingly abundantly above all that we ask or think, according to the power that works in us" (Ephesians 3:20 NKJV). Pray about it. Ask. God can do it! Think about it. Dream. God can do even more!

That means God knows who we are, what we're going through, how to help us, and he is able to do whatever he thinks is best to help us.

God is helpful. This thought seems to be everywhere you look in the Psalms. Here are a few of my favorite examples:

> I am poured out like water, and all my bones are out of joint; my heart is like wax; it is melted within my breast; [...] But you, O LORD, do not be far off! O you my help, come quickly to my aid!
>
> Psalm 22:14, 19

> As for me, I am poor and needy, but the Lord takes thought for me. You are my help and my deliverer; do not delay, O my God!
>
> Psalm 40:17

> You [the LORD] have been my help, and in the shadow of your wings I will sing for joy. My soul clings to you; your right hand upholds me.
>
> Psalm 63:7-8

If the LORD had not been my help, my soul would soon have lived in the land of silence.

Psalm 94:17

I lift up my eyes to the hills. From where does my help come? My help comes from the LORD, who made heaven and earth. He will not let your foot be moved; he who keeps you will not slumber.

Psalm 121:1-3

Add these encouraging verses to what we've already learned. First, God is everywhere. He sees everything and everyone. He knows who we are and what we are going through. Second, God knows just what to do when he sees us hurt. Third, God can do whatever he thinks he needs to do to help us. Finally, God wants to help us! That's why the Holy Spirit says, "Humble yourselves, therefore, under the mighty hand of God […] casting all your anxieties on him, because he cares for you" (1 Peter 5:6-7).

The choice is a simple one. When we suffer, we can turn *on* God and blame him for not being there, or we can turn *to* God and claim his care. He allows us to struggle because he knows it can make us stronger; but he is also right there—working in the shadows of providence—helping us get through those struggles. He may not do what we ask. He may not do what we think he should. He may take longer than we wish. ***But he is there with a heart that deeply cares.***

JOY

Agony	*Affliction*
Anguish	*Despair*
Distress	*Grief*
Grieve	*Hardship*
Hurt	*Misery*
Miserable	*Pain*
Problems	*Suffer*
Suffering	*Trials*
Tribulation	*Trouble*

On average, these words are found almost once every forty-three verses in the Bible. God's Word has a lot to say about suffering. So before we blame him for our pain, we might pause and let him explain. The long and short of what he says is this: *God is willing to let us hurt because he knows it's the secret to our happiness.*

Say what!?

Being jerked around by life is a source of joy? Agony is the path to ecstasy? "No pain, no gain"? Yeah, *riiight.* Do you really believe that? I admit that it's a hard concept for me to swallow. I can accept it, share it, and preach it when someone else hurts. But it's a lot different when sadness barges through my front door—it never bothers to knock, does it? I just want to be left alone and feel sorry for myself because God...

You finish the sentence.

I don't want to believe that something wonderful can come

from something awful. But still, if I'm going to believe the Bible, that's what it says. Here are four passages to consider:

Problems help us stay focused.

> Rejoice in hope, be patient in tribulation, be constant in prayer.
>
> Romans 12:12

Right in the middle of that short verse, there's a challenge. We are to "be patient in tribulation," or, more literally, we are to "be someone that continually remains under pressure." Problems can get pretty heavy. Sooner or later, we might want to give up, but we are instructed to keep on keeping on. Look at the verse again. On either side of this challenge, we are told how to meet it. We're encouraged to *look ahead* and hope for eternal life while we *look up* and talk to God about this life.

I'm a better person when I hurt. I think more about heaven and the hope of peace. I spend more time in prayer and find myself looking for God in the smallest developments of the day. Problems can help us cut through the clutter of life and order our thoughts on things that really matter. They help us stay on task. Our *cares* are like a *compass* that keep us focused and headed in the right direction with hearts full of joy.

Problems remind us of how blessed we are to have friends.

> I am filled with comfort. In all our affliction, I am overflowing with joy. For even when we came into Macedonia, our bodies had no rest, but we were afflicted at every turn—fighting without and fear with-

in. But God, who comforts the downcast, comforted us by the coming of Titus, and not only by his coming but also by the comfort with which he was comforted by you, as he told us of your longing, your mourning, your zeal for me, so that I rejoiced still more.

2 Corinthians 7:4-7

Read that passage again and look for Paul's terms for turmoil: *tribulation, no rest, troubled, conflicts, fears,* and *downcast.* Now, read it once more and this time see if you can find the words *comfort, comforted, consolation, joyful,* and *rejoiced.* The concern of his friends reminded Paul of how much he was loved amidst all his suffering.

There is nothing like a friend's heart when your life falls apart. They have a gentle way of cupping your tears in the palm of their hands. They are a steady shoulder, a confidential ear, and an encouraging word. "A friend loves at all times" (Proverbs 17:17; cf. 18:24). So *stress* helps us see how joyfully *blessed* we are to be loved by our friends.

Problems help us work on our faith.

Count it all joy, my brothers, when you meet trials of various kinds, for you know that the testing of your faith produces steadfastness. And let steadfastness have its full effect, that you may be perfect and complete, lacking in nothing. If any of you lacks wisdom, let him ask God, who gives generously to all without reproach, and it will be given him.

James 1:2-5

There are "trials of various kinds" we have to work through. Some are big. Some are small. Some come and go. Some last a lifetime. Some pinch. Some punch. There are:

- *Physical trials.* Some are forced to live their lives in bed, in a chair with wheels, or attached to a pair of sticks that help them get about. Some struggle to communicate their wonderful thoughts because the mechanics of speech are flawed. Some are destined to live with the memory of a younger body that doesn't function the way it used to.

- *Emotional trials.* Some carry the hidden scars of betrayal. Some can barely function inside the dark clouds of depression. Some have been overwhelmed by grief and aren't sure they will ever laugh again or give themselves permission to begin a new future.

- *Social trials.* Some feel like they are constantly interrogated by the blank stare of others. Some feel intimidated by the idea of a secret past being revealed. Some feel humiliated because a secret past has been revealed. Some feel isolated, forgotten, or ignored.

- *Financial trials.* Some are wondering where they are going to get their next meal. Some are using a roll of duct tape and a coil of bailing wire to keep their car patched together. Some are walking on sore feet from holes in their shoes because their children need clothes for school. Some are starting over because they have lost their business, their house, or their security.

Trials come in all shapes and sizes, but the Holy Spirit wants us to know that any of them can work to our advantage. They produce "steadfastness." They help us learn how to "stand fast" and become everything we can be: "perfect and complete, lacking in nothing."

Crises build *character* and, according to Paul, that's cause for joy. "We rejoice in our sufferings, knowing that suffering produces endurance, and endurance produces character" (Romans 5:3-4. Trials are a training ground (Hebrews 12:11).

Problems help strengthen our fellowship with Jesus.

> Beloved, do not be surprised at the fiery trial when it comes upon you to test you, as though something strange were happening to you. But rejoice insofar as you share Christ's sufferings, that you may also rejoice and be glad when his glory is revealed.
>
> 1 Peter 4:12-13

Several things stand out to me in these verses. First, we are not the first to "be surprised" or wonder why we have to suffer. Second, our problems aren't any worse than the "fiery trials" that have melted away the lives of others. Third, life is a university, and the things we suffer are tests we pass or fail. Finally, there is the command to be happy when we hurt because it gives us an opportunity to "share" or, more literally, "fellowship" in something Jesus experienced.

In fact, *suffer* is a key word in 1 Peter (1:11; 2:19-21, 23; 3:14, 17-18; 4:1, 13, 15-16, 19; 5:1, 9-10), and 1 Peter 4:16 is the letter's key verse: "Yet if anyone suffers as a Christian, let him not be ashamed, but let him glorify God in that name." That's what Jesus did, and that's what we get to do if we follow his example (1 Peter 2:21-23). Our *problems* can serve as a *platform* that allows us to happily show the world what God can mean to a person's life.

There's no way to escape it. We are "born to trouble" (Job 5:7; 14:1). We are going to suffer. We have no say in the matter. But what we do when we suffer is another matter. We can blame God and get *bitter*, or we can praise God and do *better*.

Have you heard about the three pots of boiling water? Carrots are in the first pot. An egg is in the second pot. Coffee grounds are in the third pot. After several minutes, the boiling water makes the hard carrots soft. It makes the soft inside of the egg hard. But the coffee grounds change the hot water into coffee.

We need to be like the coffee grounds. We don't need to get soft and lose our faith when we hurt, nor should we become hardened and calloused because we hurt. We need to transform our suffering into something that will deepen our confidence in God and broaden our influence for his glory. Remember:

- God *believes* in us.
- God *grieves* with us.
- God *cleaves* to us.
- God *achieves* great things through us.
- God *weaves* things together for us.

ACKNOWLEDGMENTS

Gratitude has been called, "The memory of a heart." So, as we come to the end of this project, I'd like to pause and gratefully remember some very special folks.

I wish to begin by thanking Michael Whitworth, owner and president of Start2Finish. For years, when he and I have been in the same area, I've asked to share some of his time and pick his brilliant mind. He has been an invaluable confidant, an encourager, and one of those amazing human beings that just makes things happen. "Michael, thank you for tightening all the nuts on to the proper bolts and making this dream a reality. Thank you for using your wonderful intellect for Jesus. Thank you for the great books you have and continue to write. (You are one of my favorite religious authors.) Most of all, thank you for being my dear friend."

I want to say, "Thank you," to Brandon Jackson and Brandon Edwards of Hidden Bridge Media. "Guys, the commitment you have given to the videos that supplement this book, has been absolutely professional and exceptional. Every time we think out-loud, work together, or film, I learn from your creative genius. You lift me up by your love for God."

To Kristy Hinson, my eagle-eye editor; Sheri Glazier, a sweet sister in Jesus; and Eloise Boyd, beloved mother-in-law, "Thank you, for the careful attention you gave to this work and the helpful thoughts you shared."

I want to thank Josh Feit, director of Evangela Creative, for crafting the logo of d&d publishing and for the intricate work given to the beautiful cover of this material.

To Diane, the love of my life and my best friend in all of this world. "Thank you, for being everything you are. The size of your heart and the gentleness of your spirit make you the most incredible person I know. I cannot imagine this world without you. Eternity will be amazing, but it will be even more so being able to spend it with you."

ABOUT THE AUTHOR

Dan Winkler has shared the story of Jesus on university campuses, in churches, convention centers, and living rooms across the U.S. His uncanny ability to unravel a biblical text and invite its meaning into our world makes him a terrific Bible study partner. You will find Dan's sensitive spirit and gentle wit to be a refreshing contribution to your pursuit of God. Dan teaches New Testament studies at Freed-Hardeman University in Henderson, Tennessee. He has preached the unsearchable riches of Christ since 1969. He and his wife, Diane, have been blessed with three sons and seven grandchildren.